AF131512

Decoding

Direct Sales &

Marketing©

*Sales tips and marketing
techniques that work (for me)*

I0490987

Frank Dappah

Author & Co-founder of
Corvus Web Services

Decoding Direct Sales and Marketing©

Sales tips and marketing techniques that work (for me)

Frank Dappah

Ostrich Publishers

Made in the U.S.A

www.ostrichpress.com

Ostrich Publishers

Charlotte, NC 28212

Copyright © 2020 by FRANK DAPPAH

Ostrich Publishers is an ardent supporter and facilitator of creativity and the free flow of communication. We aim to inspire and help bring to the public quality literary works of independent Authors around the world. Thank you for buying an authorized edition of this book and complying with copyright laws by not reproducing, scanning or distributing any part of it in any form without permission. You are supporting writers and allowing Ostrich to have the resources to continue to publish books for everyone.

ISBN: 9781655419096

For more information about products and services or perhaps to make additional purchases, visit our official website at www.ostrichpress.com. We look forward to producing and /or publishing more books in the future. You can also visit Amazon.com or anywhere books are sold to purchase any of our other works.

Dedications

To the entrepreneurs and small business folk out there starting new companies and introducing innovative solutions to help solve the world's problems.

This is for you.

OSTRICH

PUBLISHERS

www.ostrichpress.com

A COLLECTION OF LOOSELY-RELATED
USEFUL GUIDES AND TIPS TO HELP YOU
SELL MORE STUFF

DECODING
&DIRECT SALES
MARKETING

*Sales tips and
marketing techniques
that work(for me)*

FRANK DAPPAH

For Bernice, my partner, biggest fan, and the hardest working entrepreneur I know.

CONTENTS

Decoding Direct Sales and Marketing©

Sales tips and marketing techniques that work

(for me)

Read First!

Every organization's success is largely dependent on its ability to carry out a handful of its most fundamental functions. What these functions are may differ from company to company, with each having its own set of goals that need to be met.

Each firm will define success as it sees fit. For most startups, proof of concept is the main object. For those a bit further along in their evolution, customer recruitment at all cost, "traction" is the word/goal of the day.

That being said, since we all view profitability as the one true goal as entrepreneurs.

Delivering your goods and services in exchange for cash and doing so in such a way that allows you to pay your bills and stash a bit away is what we all hope for.

One can only accomplish those goals via selling, *sales*.

Always be selling

One way or the other, every organization must sell something to be able to remain viable as an entity. And the men and women within each organization who carry these ultra-important tasks are often the lifeblood of the company.

Salespeople can make or break a business.

Since you are reading this book, I can only assume that you are either a sales professional or have ambitions of soon being able to (successfully) wear that moniker.

You will want to at some point in the near future be able to say that you are a "good" sales guy or gal.

I am sure you have many questions at this point. Rest assured that I will try to shed some light on how you can master the art of selling.

Let me first say welcome and thank you for taking the time to read my book.

What to expect

The idea behind the creation of this book is pretty simple. Over the years as I have worked to build several companies and launched various products, I have always made it a point to keep a notebook, a journal of sorts.

In this journal I often find myself writing out some of my thoughts on the sales techniques and strategies that have brought me success. I will often come back and refine these notes.

I also sometimes share some of these tips on various blogs and publications.

At some point, I decided to create this book, tying together some of the sales practices that have proven profitable.

Structural integrity

I wrote this book to serve as a handy guide to any new or entry-level sales and marketing professional. A memo of sorts. A collection of useful tips to aid in your journey to becoming the best sales guru there is.

I am by no means suggesting that reading these article-form tips and guides will make you a sales expert. I wouldn't dare. As you may know "Sales and Marketing" is a very broad topic and no one man or woman can claim to have any kind of panacea for this line of work.

I am only seeking to set you on the path, as it relates to my own experiences. The format of this book is pretty straightforward. Think of it as a collection of sales and marketing articles, with each article being demarcated by a number and an introduction to help shed the light on what's in store,

Enjoy!

ONE

IDENTITY CRISIS

A genius and a salesman walk into a bar

Let it shine

In my experience, who you are as a person is a great indicator of the type of salesperson thou shall become. Biblical language aside, this is a consistent fact I have witnessed all through my career and even as an entrepreneur.

Here, I am of course talking about whether or not you are successful as a salesperson. And by "success", I mean whether or not your clients find what you provide useful enough to spend money to acquire your products and/or service.

No A#@holes allowed

You shall have to get very comfortable with who you are and not be afraid to let that show even when dealing with customers. Needless to say, if you are not a pleasant person, or if you are offensive by nature, then please! for the love of God, you are to, under no circumstance be yourself around those with who you enjoy professional dealings. All things being equal, your natural personality is the one to build on. And yes, even in sales.

We all have this image of the ideal salesperson being pushy and obnoxious. Somewhere along the line, this became our mental picture of sales folks.

Perhaps we got this idea from all the corny '80's, '90's and early 2000's movies about men and women stapled to their cubicles selling stocks and bonds.

We have allowed movies like the 2000 hit movie Boiler Room and Michael Douglas' hit movie Wall Street to define our understanding of what it means or looks like to be "in sales". Folks calling unsuspecting consumers on the phone, talking loud and fast.

This is not reality. Sure, there are some sales folks who act like this. Lord knows I have met a lot of them. The thing is, they are typically not very good at what they do.

As the saying goes

"People buy from people they like, period" or something to that effect. I have found this statement and many others like it to be true in one way or another.

Your "best" customers are going to be the ones who know you, in other words, have done business with you before.

Trust you, meaning they trust that you know what you are doing or at the very least, trust that you have their best interests at heart. And like you.

This truth does not mean that you have to try to become "best friends" with your customers. I have watched as many new sales folks try and fail at this very hard to watch or listen to task. The best way to accomplish all three is to just be yourself.

This, in my view, is the best version of you you can be. I happen to think that everyone is super interesting in their own unique way and that if you stop trying to be someone else, interested parties will be in for a delight as they uncover the mountain of complexities, quirks, and idiosyncrasies that is you, This, I am 100 percent sure of.

I am socially awkward

And I have to say, this has not stopped me from being successful in sales and business as a whole. As they say "success is a journey, not a destination" true. So, let me clarify.

By "success" I mean, me and my awkward self have managed to first build a successful insurance business, then a profitable software and services business, plus a few profitable investments in real estate and a nice collection of books -insert shameless plug: now selling on Amazon and everywhere else books are sold.

Sorry about that. I plug my books so much it has become a reflex.

Anyway, what was I saying? Oh yeah. So, my point is, I have been able to get a few wins under my belt. Wins that required me selling stuff to consumers and businesses. Hell, I started out doing door-to-door sales and I am as awkward as they come. I did not let that stop me though.

In fact, those who do business with me seem to enjoy that corner of the little bit of personality I have. I am very inquisitive, OCD, and have been told I have no filter, which has made for some very funny sales calls over the years.

My point is, I am who I am at all times. I am this way because, in my mind, I have no other options. I like to think I am an overall positive guy, so all my quirks are just me being me, but not in any negative way.

Who are you?

The first step to being you is knowing who you are. This is easier said than done for many folks. Some of us are afraid to be who we are because we think who we are is not good enough.

Others simply have no idea who they are. This is important because it will be the thing that will define you as a sales professional. This reality and the discovery of oneself will define you as a sales guy or gal.

In my view, you can be one of three kinds of sales professionals, and you can make a very good living in either case. Of course, the challenge of self-discovery is one that I cannot help you with. That is between you, your faith leader and your therapist. I can, however, break down all three versions of sales folk I have seen in the field to help you work some things out within your soul.

Suits

Have you ever seen it? If you have, then you obviously know what I am talking about. But if you haven't, then let me give you some background: Suits is *USA Network's* courtroom comedy-drama starring Gabriel Macht. The first few seasons had Megan, Duchess of Sussex Markle starring as the incomparable Rachel Zane, a young up and coming, impressionable lawyer.

Cast Season 5 in 2019 | Suits

In any case, I use this show, or more specifically, the three main original characters frequently to showcase the three kinds of salespeople there are, In my view of course.

You just got litt-up

Played by Rick Hoffman, Louis Litt specializes in financial transactions. Seeing as how the show centers on the goings and comings of a corporate law firm.

Litt is the resourceful type of salesperson. The Competent one.

He is my favorite character on the show. I like Louis because I see myself in him a little bit. He is strange as hell, not very good with people but he is the only one on the show as far as the bunch goes that is consistently dependable.

He knows his stuff, does the research, is super meticulous and works hard to earn his spot every single day.

Maybe this is why (spoiler alert) he later takes the helm as the managing partner when Jessica leaves. Who is Jessica? Forget I brought her up. Let's move on.

Sure, Louis has some deep personal issues, which helps produce some of the show's funniest moments.

Louis is not the kind of guy you would have a beer with if he was your Lawyer, but you can bet he will get the job done when it counts.

Rest assured that there is no way your ex is getting full custody of you're the Iguana as long as Louis is on the case.

Rick Hoffman (Louis Litt)

What would Harvey do?

I think we are all familiar with the Harvey type. Spector Played by Macht is the star of the show. Harvey is the stereotypical sales guy.

He is not very good at what he does and often lets his emotions cloud his judgement. Oh, and he can be very unprofessional.

That said, he is super effective.

Why? Because where he fails at being a subject matter expert or in my view consistent, he makes up for it by being the one thing that trumps all when dealing directly with people: *Likeable*.

He is witty, handsome and super confident. What you come to find out as you watch the show is that he has had to become these things to make up for the fact that he is no Mike or Louis.

He leans on his strengths. He is a Salesman's salesman. And by doing so, he finds himself being the one that most clients and potential clients want to deal with when they solicit the services of the firm.

He is essentially the face of the organization. The business-generator. The Closer if you will.

Gabriel Macht (Harvey Specter)

The Genius

The third character is Mike Ross. Played by the young Patrick Adams, Rachel's love interest in the first few seasons.

Mike is the super smart kind of salesperson. The kind of guy who can solve problems at the drop of a dime, even ones that are not typically seen in his line of work. A true out-of-the-box thinker.

He is a fast learner, a great resource as he devours information at a pace that goes beyond what most of his contemporaries are capable of.

He is fun to be around, likeable as well but shines when clients have complex issues that require a fresh new approach. On the show, Ross' tendency to cross lines becomes a bit of an issue. One that lands him in jail.

Sales folks who have a bit of a Mike in them should be sure to learn to push the envelope but not break the law.

Patrick Adams AKA Mike Ross and Meghan Markle

TWO

REJECTION SENSITIVE

DYSPHORIA (RSD)

Overcoming the fear of rejection in sales

It's only natural

We, humans, have retained a great deal of the traits our ancestors cultivated and displayed in the earlier days of our existence as a species.

2.5 million years of evolution have done very little to eradicate some of our most primal of instincts.

For one, and as it relates to our organizing principles, we love community. We, for better or worse are naturally drawn to others like ourselves.

We have lived in small communities since we walked the earth. We hunted in groups very early on, and when we became growers and cultivators, we did so in groups, and still do today.

Even those in the corporate world, for the most part prefer working alongside a community of people.

This part of our being is crucial to our survival. Remember, we have managed to slay every single natural predator armed with nothing but our wits and our ability to collaborate with one another. Evidence of our need for community goes all the way back to the caves of North Africa where the story of the human genus started.

Earlier on, as we braved all manner of bad weather conditions out in the wilderness, disease, and numerous predatory creatures, being exiled from the group, the community, the tribe literally meant your death.

The generally accepted orthodoxy among most phycologists is that this was the genesis of our fear of being ostracized, criticized and/or rejected. For most people. This fear transcends most fears, even death.

The fear of rejection does not have to get in the way of success in sales and marketing.

Open for business

So, you just signed the lease on your new office space and moved in. Or perhaps you just started a new position as a Salesperson. It is now time to get out there and start selling. It is imperative to the survival of your new business that you are able to attract new customers.

Everyone you know in the biz keeps telling you to go out and "Prospect", but the thought of walking up and talking to folks you don't know scares the heck out of you.

You are even unsure of which of your LinkedIn contacts to contact via email to let them know what you are up to and perhaps get some facetime with them to talk about your new position and how you can help them personally or professionally. " Will I be coming off as pushy or desperate? " Should I only reach out to folks I am very familiar with?": You ask yourself.

If this sounds like you, then you are not alone. Many new business owners and/or sales professionals out there are terrified of the idea of being "rejected" when trying to sell their products or services to total strangers and even friends and family.

"Follow these rules and you'll have mad bread to breakup"

A spoonful of sugar

After over a decade in sales. I have come to learn a few things. I have realized that no matter what your business is or what line of work you are in, when selling to either businesses or professionals, there are a few points to consider.

Realizing these truths and using these steps as a guide will help you reach your goals and overcome many challenges associated with your fear of failure and rejection.

It's not personal

Let's face it, humans are - for the most part, emotional beings. This is what makes us more advanced and more sophisticated than the other creatures on this earth.

Emotional motivation is what caused

Galileo to dedicate his life to exploring the cosmos. It is what would drive Jean-Michel Basquiat to produce some of the most fascinating works ever seen in the art world. Emotions, however, sometimes lead us astray.

Such is the case when it comes to sales. We invest a lot of emotional capital into each and every outcome of the sales process.

We get crushed when our prospects end up not buying from us. Remember, Sales is really a numbers game and our prospects may have a million reasons why our product is not "right" for them at that time.

Your job is to play the odds- having a high number of prospects at a time so as to end up with an acceptable amount of closed sales after each sales period.

It's not about you

In my experience, and maybe I am being a tad bit cynical, but most of the kick-ass salespeople I have ever met in my life tend to be ego-driven, self-absorbed blowhards.

They tend to see the sales process as a performance with them smack dead in the middle of it all as the star.

The reality is, folks, buy from you because they like dealing with you, but also because they have a genuine need for your product or service.

Focusing your attention on the customers' needs helps you serve them better. You get to anticipate their needs and wants by paying attention to what their experiences are like.

Setup a Follow-up system

Ok, so the prospect you have been "working" for weeks finally told you that she is going with a competitor's product. Or, perhaps she said, "Now is not a good time". Try not to take this personally.

After all, your prospect is human, and they may have some stuff going on in their lives at the time that makes it impossible to buy from you. Heck, they may simply not have the cash to buy your custom dog sweaters at the moment.

The delayed closure is an inevitable part of sales. It is best to construct a system to help follow-up with some of the folks who were not ready to buy from you in the past. Simply ask if you could follow up with them in say a few weeks and keep these contacts in rotation to follow-up. You will be amazed at how much of a difference a few months makes.

Open communication, open wallets

No matter what your product or service is, if you are in sales for yourself, your clients are a goldmine of opportunity and endless revenue potential. Ok, let me break that down.

If you are an entrepreneur, keep in mind that while you work hard to sell your customers one product or another, there are various other peripheral products and services you can offer your clients.

Wells Fargo, the Banking powerhouse is known for working hard to sell their clients as many products as they can, per customer. Their general business ethos is to own as much a share of a customer's wallet as possible. This strategy has helped transform the San Francisco, CA bank into a household name.

Controversies aside, Wells has been very successful at extracting as much revenue per customer with this strategy.

You too can imitate this overall plan. You will be able grow your revenue and reduce your marketing costs by approaching your sales process this way.

Constant communication with your customers, becoming a resource for them will help put you in the know as it relates to their other needs. It helps to create an information extraction plan: Try to create a questionnaire. One that will help guide you to better understand the overall needs of your clients and how you can better serve them by offering more products based on their unique needs.

Each time you come into contact with each customer, be sure to ask one of your questions, helping you draw a roadmap of your customers needs.

THREE

TECHNOCRACY NOW

*Embracing technology for the sake of
your business*

Seeking out tools

Sales, like any other job function or business activity, is in constant evolution. If you ever visit online destinations like TechCrunch (one of my favorites) or vator.tv, you will be simply amazed at how many different tech tools and platforms are rolled out every day.

Apps and gizmos developed by entrepreneurs just like you, from all corners of the globe.

I am a tech junky, a technophile if you will. I am constantly on the lookout for tools coming online that I can use to improve my business in some incremental way, at the very least.

I am constantly telling folks I do business with to adopt a similar set of practices. That is to say, to be on the lookout at all times for new tech to improve their bottom lines, make production faster, help serve more customers, and so on.

As you read this book, I wouldn't be doing my job if I didn't encourage you to do the same.

A jungle out there

If you at times feel simply overwhelmed with all the various tools out there, I get it. There are about a thousand tools launched every day, it seems. I personally think this kind of diversity in tools and apps helps improve upon exiting ones and help drive the cost to acquire most tools down. That being said, I can see how you might get lost in the sea of software applications out there. I can certainly understand if you are not sure where to start.

Right tool for the right job

Let me try to help. There are some basic software applications that any sales professional with customers or clients should have. I mean, if nothing else, you should have a robust customer relationship management (CRM) application to help manage your customer information as well as your daily tasks.

You should, of course, have some kind of email tracking system like Yesware, especially if you exchange a lot of emails with your customers, employees or colleagues. If you mostly engage in outbound telemarketing, then you certainly want to have some kind of automated outbound telephony system.

These are but a few of the most basic software tools that I believe will make your life a whole lot easier.

Campaign management

In the areas of outbound/inbound call campaigns and text message-based marketing management, Callhub (callhub.io) to me is the "must-have" tool. I wouldn't be able to do my job and run my business effectively without this dynamic telephony application.

The program has many features that appeal to folks such as myself. Those of us who do most of our prospecting and execute our customer service duties via telephone calls and text messaging.

As phone-based sales folks, we need to be able to contact a large number of consumers and/or business prospective clients to make our pitch or set up times to meet with our prospects.

At an average conversion rate of 1-3% for telephone prospecting, one must indeed be able to call over 100 contacts a day to be able to have a sizeable number of hot prospects in your pipeline at all times.

This can be a daunting task, especially for folks new to sales without the use of technology.

I am always surprised to come across sales folks who insist on eliminating the use of technology from their businesses and are shocked when their output, and by extension bottom lines seem to shrink as a result.

One must fully embrace technology in sales, especially when it comes to being able to contact a whole bunch of folks in a relatively short amount of time.

We also need efficient ways to manage our outbound and inbound campaigns and be able to scale our operations when needed. Callhub supports all these requirements and more.

Th e service is pretty easy-to-use and pay-as-you-go. Which makes it very affordable for folks just starting out in sales.

"Features built for conversations that matter"

Call Center

With a simple, easy-to-use user interface, the app provides you with the power to automate the repetitive parts of phone calls with their super-efficient outbound call center.

Multiple automated dialers to match every calling requirement. Surveying tools to track responses. With unlimited agent seats, which makes running a multi-agent business easier. Your salespeople can log into their accounts from anywhere in the world to execute their campaign requirements.

You will have the power to allocate various campaigns to different agents in different departments, product mixes, levels of agent maturity, etc.

Getting your message out

With Callhub, you can Send pre-recorded audio messages to landlines and cellphones. Play a message, record audio or transfer the call based on the digit that is pressed after answer.

Create dynamic messages announcing the introduction of new services and products with ease.

Their Voice Broadcasting feature is great when you are looking to deliver a message with various value points to a large group of people and then allowing folks to call a specific phone number for more information, or to connect with you and/or your salespeople live.

This tool is also great for making robocalls on behalf of political candidates or to solicit donations for charitable organizations.

Busybodies and Techies

Do you offer your products to folks who are a bit busier than the average person? Or perhaps you sell to a younger, more tech-savvy audience.

If you do, then you understand how important it is to be able to communicate with your prospects via text message.

Did you know that though only 25% of marketers in the U.S use text messaging as a means of communicating with their clients and customers, over 65% report being satisfied with this means of communication?

70% of consumers in the United States

say they appreciate getting texts or emails from healthcare providers. 75% of people would like to have offers sent to them via SMS.

Account management

Goes without saying, the key to success in sales is great customer service, and the key to that - success in sales- is impeccable record-keeping. In fact, with all the various tools out there to help you do just that, there is really no reason to leave this particular area uncovered.

Repeat business

As you acquire more and more customers, you will start to see three things happen: 1) You will get contacted frequently by these folks who are looking for assistance with one thing or another.

This first kind of inbound call or inbound request will either be for assistance with a product or service you have already sold, or your client will be looking to inquire about another solution you may offer, or they believe you offer.

Referrals

The second type of call will certainly be from other folks who know some of your clients and are looking for assistance with a product or solution you offer based on a recommendation from your current customer. The coveted referral. In either case, keeping "good" records, AKA Customer accounts, will go a long way to help you keep track of it all.

A few recommendations

As I was saying before, there are various customer relationship management tools to help navigate this particular challenge. Some are pretty basic and straightforward, offering features that help you upload customer documents, input customer details, notes, and other pertinent customer information and so on. Others offer a bit more bang for your buck.

These advanced CRM tools tend to go beyond the everyday features and help you build deeper, more profitable relationships with your customers.

That being said, here are some of the software applications I use to help manage my customer data and interactions.

An Oldie but goodie

I do use "Skype for business" for business calls. I know what you are thinking: "That's pretty basic" and believe me, I know.

I like using skype because you get to keep various phone numbers and you also get to send text (SMS) messages as well as make and receive calls from the same interface.

You even get to see both kinds of conversations – SMS messages and calls made and received - with customers from the same window.

You can start video calls with customers, save their names and numbers so you know who is calling at all times, etc.

Skype is also widely used overseas, making it a perfect tool for those of us who have a global network of contractors, employees, etc.

The app has really improved over the past five years or so after the Microsoft acquisition and if you haven't looked at it in a while, I really encourage you to check out Skype for business.

Podio

Podio is an all-in-one project management and customer management solution.

I especially like Podio for its versatility and price-point.

The app offers many features including tools to help manage your tasks, share files between your teams, manage your "Workspaces" if you have more than one company or business line and many more.

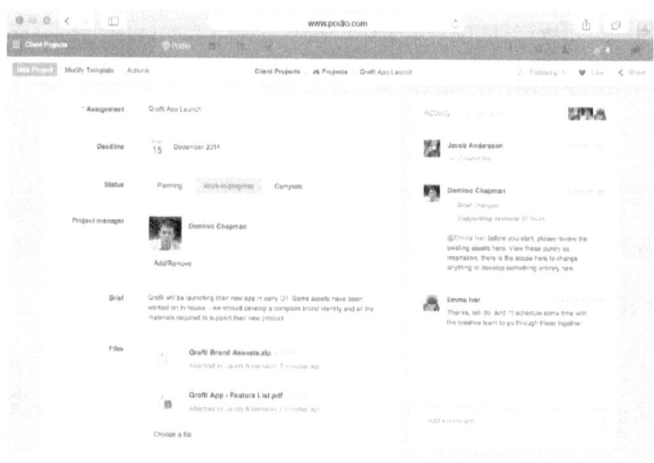

Clearbit

Clearbit is perfect for Sales professionals who deal with or sell to other businesses (B2B). The app is great for finding the emails addresses of professionals at other firms.

The app's smooth interface allows you to search for email addresses and send out emails without leaving your inbox.

Recapped

Recapped lets sales reps easily create professional deal pages that impress their prospects, guide them through the sales cycle, and track their engagement.

This makes it easy to drive deals forward by having everyone and everything on a single page, with clear next steps and action items.

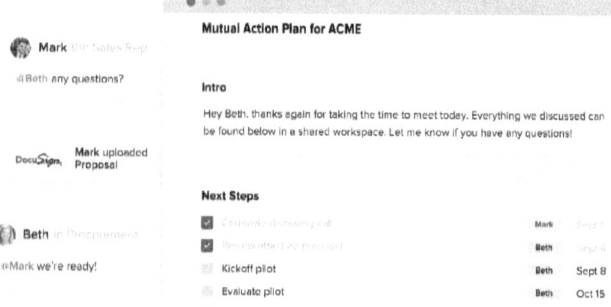

Mark *Dir Sales Rep*

@Beth any questions?

DocuSign. **Mark** uploaded Proposal

Beth *at Procurement*

@Mark we're ready!

Mutual Action Plan for ACME

Intro

Hey Beth, thanks again for taking the time to meet today. Everything we discussed can be found below in a shared workspace. Let me know if you have any questions!

Next Steps

☑	Schedule discovery call	Mark	Sept 1
☑	Demonstrate live demoed	Beth	Sept 4
☐	Kickoff pilot	Beth	Sept 8
☐	Evaluate pilot	Beth	Oct 15
☐	Go live date	Beth	Nov 8

FOUR

REFERRAL GENERATION MATRIX (RGM)

How to generate referrals from existing clients

Holy grail

One of the most effective ways to drive sales and increase profitability within your business is through a referral program or referrals.

Sure, there are many ways one can go about trying to entice their existing customer base to refer them to their friends and family members. There are also a whole bunch of software applications that can make soliciting and collecting customer referrals an easy-to-implement exercise.

Many that can be easily adapted and executed, but which ones really produce the results you seek?

"According to the New York Times, around 65% of new business/customers generally comes from referrals".

Many of these all-in-one referral programs are easy to deploy but fail to drive the kind of engagement needed to make any referral program, especially one used by a small business worth the time and resources needed to get it off the ground.

Referral programs, when implemented correctly, are ideal at generating word-of-mouth buzz for your business.

Your newfound brand recognition will go a long way to help you generate sales and a healthy ROI.

"Referred customers are about 18% more likely to stay rather than other customers. (Straight Talk about Word-of-mouth Marketing – Wharton"

That being said, here are three ways, according to small business loan platform Kabbage, one can help make their referral program a success.

Use enticing relevant incentives

Value, like beauty, is in the eyes of the beholder. One man (or woman's) art is another's " I am not sure what I am looking at". People gravitate towards and will invest their time and money in things they deem valuable. Keep this in mind as you work to build your referral program and only offer stuff that your customers will find valuable as incentives.

Then and only then will they take the time to follow the steps needed to refer their friends and family to your business.

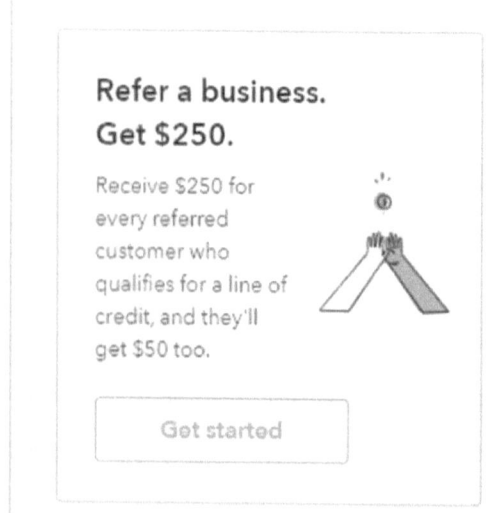

**Refer a business.
Get $250.**

Receive $250 for
every referred
customer who
qualifies for a line of
credit, and they'll
get $50 too.

Get started

You may want to offer both customers and
their referrals some sort of incentive. The trick
is to think about your brand and business type
before settling on a reward because if people
don't think the reward is worth it, they likely
won't put in the effort to share the word about
what you do and how your products and
services can help improve the lives of those
they come across or know.

Offers to motivate referrals

Cash/Gift Card – This is great for all business types but especially for those who sell a one time buy item, like a car or mattress.

In store credit – If you have a business where people may buy from you multiple times, like an ecommerce or service-type business, you can offer credit or a discount. This can keep customers happy enough to keep spending money at your business.

Special perks – Think of a VIP club, or a group who gets offered all the best or new products first. You could even offer special treatment for referring members – like a special parking spot or an early access party.

Entry for a drawing – This can be a good one for any business but can be even more rewarding for businesses with repeat customers as they will be incentivized to purchase more if it means they will acquire another entry.

However, the reward has to be pretty outstanding in this sense, like concert tickets or something else of value.

Provide a clear message

This can't be mentioned enough. If there is any confusion on what the customer or their referral has to do to complete the steps required to unlock your reward(s), they will likely give up before trying.

So be sure to provide very clear and direct messaging.

Don't scare them with a bunch of confusing wording, or a long list of jumbled instructions. It's important to remember that the more convenient it is for someone, the more likely they will be to do you the favor of referring.

No one is required to refer, but if the messaging is clear, and the process isn't overly complicated... You're likely to have customer happily refer you.

Keep the process simple

If you make the process of referring overcomplicated, it can deter people from sharing.

So, you'll want to be sure that once your customers are in the zone to refer, they are able to do so quickly and easily.

The process needs to be convenient for the referring party.

Meaning, let them know what you want, and give them the breadcrumbs to complete the desired action.

To make it even easier, allow the user to refer right from the same page.

By offering a quick email message or social media sharing option directly from the landing page, users can complete the desired action without having to jump through hoops.

And the same should be said for the new

customer's experience. They shouldn't have to jump through hoops either.

The easiest way to do this is to use cookies that can tie the referrer directly to the referring customer as soon as the referral link is clicked.

The Fiverr referral program is a good example of this. They offer an easy-to-refer form for the customer.

The customer has a few options for referring as well, including email and social media.

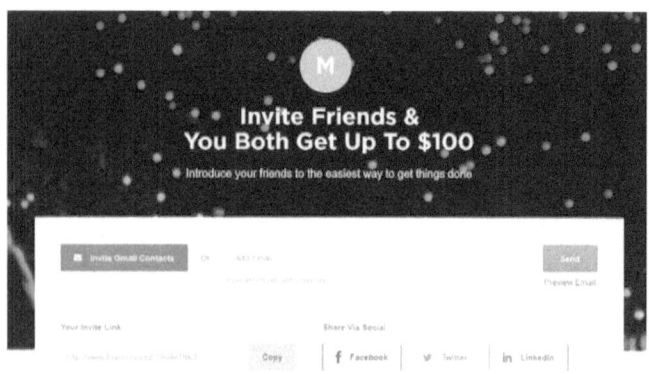

The referred customer receives a nice message, followed by a clear call to action.

 **is tired of keeping Fiverr a secret.**

Discover the easiest way to hire online freelancers and get 20% off your first order.
From marketing to tech, complete all your projects on Fiverr. On budget. On time.

FIVE

ATTRITION PREVENTION MEASURES (APM)

MEASURES (APM)

How to improve customer loyalty and satisfaction

Eye on the prize

Every business owner knows that you can never have enough paying customers.

Customer acquisition is ranked very high among entrepreneurs across different industries.

While most of a firm's resources are spent on acquiring new customers, it is important to realize that creating brand loyalty is a very inexpensive way to increase sales while maintaining a relatively low-cost structure.

There are several things you can do to reduce attrition among customers.

Create Loyalty programs

This is pretty self-explanatory.

Build some kind of loyalty program that rewards customers who shop regularly or have been with your company for a while.

This could be in the form of discounts or free stuff.

Host Flash Sales

This is very effective. Occasionally send out invitations to customer-only sales events on your website.

This lets customers know they are appreciated and encourages them to shop more often with you.

Create curated content

Although this strategy might be a bit time-consuming, it is well worth it if executed properly.

Create a customer only section on your site where you publish video tutorials, guides, etc. Specifically, for certain segments of customers.

An example would be, creating DIY videos for folks who buy hardware and construction items.

Resolve issues quickly

Great customer service is hard to find these days, as we all move to self-serve experiences. This phenomenon presents the perfect opportunity for you to stand out.

Add a human touch to addressing your customer concerns.

Be active on social media

Social media is an awesome way to interact with your customers in a natural way. Engage with customers on your various social media platforms. Answer questions and address concerns this way.

 # SIX

BOGO AND BEYOND

Grow your bottom line with Bundles

Ask any Marketer or entrepreneur, especially folks who primarily sell online and through other digital channels, and they will tell you how difficult it is to cut through the noise these days.

Business owners and entrepreneurs such as yourself now find themselves in a constant struggle with the likes of Facebook and Netflix for the attention of their potential customers.

I mean, back in the early 2000's when eCommerce was just starting to pick up, and SAAS was not really a thing, things were a bit more straightforward: You build a simple HTML website, integrate a shopping cart and sell your stuff. That was it!

Even for folks in other kinds of businesses and industries, things were a bit less convoluted. News media outlets didn't need to work as hard as they do now to get us to tune in and watch or listen to their broadcasts on the radio and television.

Folks like myself had no issue moving things online and trying to make a profit while doing it. There were very few competitors in the game. Now things have gotten a bit more complicated. There are online stores all over the place, selling all kinds of stuff, at all kinds of low prices.

In the insurance sales business, we must now compete with various online destinations that help consumers compare and buy all types of insurance plans directly online.

In the online retail space, even The big box stores at some point got in on the action, further thinning out profit margins for smaller operators.

In the Software space, larger firms like Oracle and Apple have decided to fully enter the Software-as-a-service space with a "Take no prisoners " approach. It really is hard out here for a pimp.

Allow me to share one of the techniques I have used in the past to generate more sales, signups, etc.

Bundles. Bundles, Bundles

Here is the thing: Customers love bundles. Why? Because bundles offer value.

Most folks would love to and will jump at a chance to get all they need in one place, for a simple easy-to-understand price.

I am talking about bundles now because as you plan and set up your direct sales and marketing system, especially when you begin to automate a whole lot of your basic tasks and processes and embark on expanding your customer base and sales numbers, you will start to look for ways to get your target audience to respond to your messages.

Just like how we talked about using using the various technology tools out there to help you grow your business and simplify more of your complex tasks in previous chapters, you will want to think of ways in which you can engage your audience.

The use of bundles, regardless of the nature of your product offering will help present enormous value to your customers. You will also be helping your customers realize their need for convenience be eliminating further actions on their part to acquire other complementary products.

Bundles are used heavily in eCommerce by the likes of Amazon.com and Wal-Mart, and some brick-and-mortar establishments.

I would, however, recommend that you find creative ways to bundle some of your services and products to help boost customer engagement and sales.

The key is to offer complementary products as bundles at slightly discounted prices compared to those products or services being purchased separately.

Amazon does a great job at offering bundles that make sense. Of course, they do so by using AI technology to determine which products their customers are more likely to buy as a bundle.

Frequently Bought Together

Price for all three: $55.65

[Add all three to Cart] [Add all three to Wish List]

Show availability and shipping details

☑ **This item:** Burt's Bees Naturally Ageless Night Creme, 2-Ounce Jar $18.20

☑ Burt's Bees Naturally Ageless Line Smoothing Eye Cream, 0.5 Ounces $17.16

☑ Burt's Bees Naturally Ageless Line Diminishing Day Lotion, 2 Ounces $20.29

They also use historical purchase data to help create bundles to offer to their new customers.

I love receiving emails from Amazon offering bundles.

I always open those emails to see how I can purchase what I need at a discount.

SEVEN

THE PERPETUAL HUNT

How consistent prospecting can grow your sales business

Coffee and tea

My parents were raised in a farming community. My paternal grandparents were large scale farmers and made a living growing selling cash crops like coffee, tea and wheat to the Kenyan government for export.

The one thing that farming teaches you is that there is a time and a season for everything. A time to prepare the soil, the right time to sow the seeds, the right amount of water to germinate the seeds and the right amount of sunshine and rain to grow a "good" crop. The crop has to be lovingly taken care of, fed nutrients, and every threat of pestilence has to be dealt with and eliminated. As a farmer, you do everything you can to give nature the opportunity to produce a bountiful harvest.

The harvest is the big payoff, it is the culmination of all the hard work, toil and money invested. What the harvest represents to the farmers is their livelihood, the ability to pay workers and the money to invest in another crop the following year.

Sales is very similar to farming in the sense that, the harvest is when the customer finally signs on to do business with you. Just like in farming, a series of steps or activities have to be performed in the right order and executed at the right time to ensure a bountiful harvest.

It all starts with prospecting

The lifeblood of sales is prospecting. Prospecting to sales is what seed is to the farmer. Seeds like prospects represent possibilities. The more prospects you have, the more likely you will make sales.

Therefore, if there is one skill that salespeople have to master, it is how to prospect, because mastering this skill is directly related to the success or failure of your sales organization. Now the good news about prospecting is, it is a skill, and therefore anyone can learn it and master it if they choose to.

So, what is prospecting exactly?

Prospecting is the practice of looking for likely and potential customers for your product or business and making an offer to them.

The first question that comes to mind to

most salespeople when they come across that definition is where do you find likely and potential customers? The answer is in the product or service you offer.

Think about it for a second, who is your core customer? What age ranges are they in, are they baby boomers, generation x, y, z, millennials? What income bracket they are in, what is their marital status, what gender are they? Do they live in the city, or in a rural area?

Try and really and understand your customer as much as possible. Ask them how they use your product or service and what it represents to them emotionally.

Really try to understand your customers on a molecular level, what makes them tick?

I work in Insurance, I started off in life insurance with very few personal viable contacts and my wife and I have had to build a book of business customer by customer through trial and error. In the pursuit of selling insurance, we started noticing that we were having more success with a certain type of customer over the other.

Our customers are in the market for final expense insurance. This is insurance for funerals, final medical expenses and small legacies for their families. Naturally because of the product offering, our customers are older people between the ages of 55-85, and the more experience we had in this market, we realized that we had more success with women in that age demographic who had older children and had some grandchildren and whose income ranged from 20-50k a year and resided in a rural area.

Insurance for this group of people was motivated by love of their families. It represented security and peace of mind. Their motivation was, that they did not want to be a burden on their family financially in any way with regards to their final expenses. They wanted to leave a little money for their loved ones, and they did not want their families to be worried about paying any outstanding bills that they would have upon their passing. Insurance to them represented a solution and a way to keep caring for their family's needs when they were ultimately called home.

Find more of the same....

Using demographics as a guide to find more people that are in the same boat, a tribe of sorts with the same common issues, becomes easier once you know what you are looking for and where to find them.

Once you find a group with similar demographics as your ideal customer, the next natural step is to contact them, make a value offering and see who responds.

There are specific ways on how to contact leads and how to make a value offering, but for the sake of simplicity, the most important step in prospecting is to really figure out who buys from you and try and get a list of more people with similar traits and offer your product.

You will have a higher chance of people from the list buying your product or service from someone in a similar demographic as your customer than just randomly marketing to anyone..really...including friends and family.

In my business, getting to know our customer demographic, was the thing that shifted our business forward, it allowed us to look for similar people with matching profiles and similar life circumstances, and there we were able to find our market, people truly in need of our product.

And for me, finally a way to serve in some little way and provide a solution to some gnawing problem that hadn't been settled yet.

Repeat daily

Prospecting is a practice. You get better at sales when you create the opportunity to make more sales.

A bulk of your sales are directly related to the amount of prospecting that you do and the easiest way to prospect is to do it every single day.

I say do it every day because that is what works for me.

As a salesperson, you will typically find yourself with a lot of free time during your business hours.

Most salespeople's schedules are not regimented or restrictive at all. Not in the least bit. And for good reason.

You will have ample flexibility as to what to do with your time during the workday so long as you deliver the numbers. That is if you are an independent sales agent or are in outside sales.

Unfortunately, if you are not disciplined, you will hang yourself with the free time.

You will wait until the last minute to try and pull a rabbit out of a hat every single time.

Most people in this line of work do so to the detriment of their jobs or business overall.

Let me also say that if this non-structured workday works for you, that is perfectly fine too. I have, over the years come across a few very productive, very successfully businesspeople who thrive in chaotic unpredictable work environments.

I just know that it does not work for most people.

Most people need a system, a process to get somewhat consistent results and for that you need discipline.

Discipline does not come easy to me, so to make it work for me, and my personality I have to schedule my prospecting time daily.

Block off some time and communicate with people, introduce yourself and what you do to at least 100 people a day. Why 100? I know everybody has heard the old line that sales is a numbers game. Well that is still true.

In my experience, when you are starting out, it takes 100 calls to make 2- 3 life insurance appointments. These are typically folks who agree to sit and talk with you about their life insurance needs.

It took, and still does take 100 tries to get a yes.

The longer you do it (make calls/contact), the better you get at it and the better your conversion rate.

I recommend setting a goal of making 2 appointments a day in order to get your sales momentum going.

About the author

FRANK DAPPAH

Frank is a serial entrepreneur and hobbyist. Over the last ten years, he, along with his wife and business partner, Bernice have founded and operate various businesses.

The couple started out by starting an independent insurance agency.

A business they still own and operate. Their agency opened its doors in 2011. The same year they met.

The company was initially started by Frank. Gathoni soon joined as a partner.

They grew the company into a profitable venture and later started Corvus (www.corvus.website), a software business that was started as a way for them to build software solutions for their insurance business.

Soon, other businesses were subscribing to what has become numerous software applications.

The couple is currently investors and

partners in various other business ventures. They spend most of their time in Charlotte, North Carolina, where they live. Frank is originally from Ghana, West Africa where he was born and raised till he moved to Philadelphia, Pennsylvania.

Frank has always had an entrepreneurial spirit. Seeing his father build, along with his mother, the family business.

He always wanted to start his own company, and soon did after college and a few years in the corporate world. Today, Frank spends his time running his business and writing business and sales books whenever he gets some free time.

He has, till date published over eight business books.

All his books can be purchased at www.ostrichpress.com or on Amazon.com.

Author's other books

Recurring Revenue: A Practical Guide to help you launch your very own Software-as-a-service business

PIXIE DUST: How to Convince Investors to Invest in Your Business

Startup Monday: How to tackle some of the often-overlooked challenges you will face while trying to grow your Startup company

Adventures in
MARKETING
AUTOMATION

Out-of-the-box tips, concepts, and ideas on how to use
Robotics**, **Artificial Intelligence**, and **Automation *to
reach a wider audience.*

FRANK DAPPAH

ADVENTURES IN MARKETING
AUTOMATION

A COLLECTION OF LOOSELY-RELATED
USEFUL GUIDES AND TIPS TO HELP YOU
SELL MORE STUFF

DECODING
&DIRECT SALES
MARKETING

Sales tips and
marketing techniques
that work(for me)

FRANK DAPPAH

A COLLECTION OF LOOSELY-RELATED
USEFUL GUIDES AND TIPS TO HELP YOU
SELL MORE STUFF

DECODING
&DIRECT SALES
MARKETING

*Sales tips and
marketing techniques
that work(for me)*

FRANK DAPPAH

Ostrich Publishers

Charlotte, NC 28212

Copyright © 2020 by FRANK DAPPAH

Ostrich Publishers is an ardent supporter and facilitator of creativity and the free flow of communication. We aim to inspire and help bring to the public quality literary works of independent Authors around the world. Thank you for buying an authorized edition of this book and complying with copyright laws by not reproducing, scanning or distributing any part of it in any form without permission. You are supporting writers and allowing Ostrich to have the resources to continue to publish books for everyone.

ISBN: 9781655419096

For more information about products and services or perhaps to make additional purchases, visit our official website at www.ostrichpress.com. We look forward to producing and /or publishing more books in the future. You can also visit Amazon.com or anywhere books are sold to purchase any of our other works.

While the author has made every effort to provide accurate telephone numbers, internet addresses, and other contact information at the time of publication of this book, neither the publisher nor the author assumes any responsibility for errors or for changes that occur after publication. In addition, the author assumes no responsibility for the accuracy of any information presented here in this book.

A COLLECTION OF LOOSELY-RELATED
USEFUL GUIDES AND TIPS TO HELP YOU
SELL MORE STUFF

DECODING
&DIRECT SALES
MARKETING

Sales tips and marketing techniques that work(for me)

FRANK DAPPAH

We are Ostrich!

Visit OSTRICH Publishers at
www.ostrichpress.com to check out the rest of
our published books.

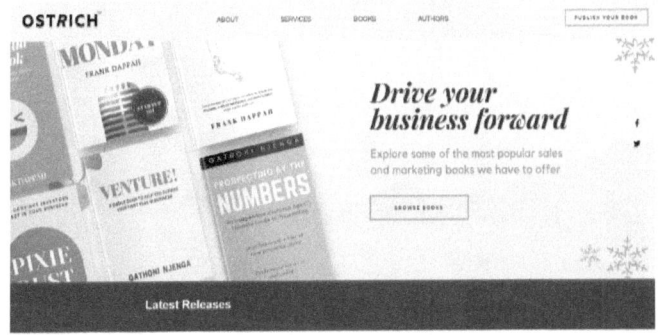

OSTRICH™

Ostrich Publishers

Made in the U.S.A

www.ostrichpress.com

www.ingramcontent.com/pod-product-compliance
Lightning Source LLC
Chambersburg PA
CBHW021422210526
45463CB00001B/497